RICHMOND

TRAVEL GUIDE
2024

Uncover the City's Unexpected Charm,

Where Southern Hospitality Meets

Creative Energy

JENNIFER JAMES

TABLE OF CONTENT

MAP OF RICHMOND

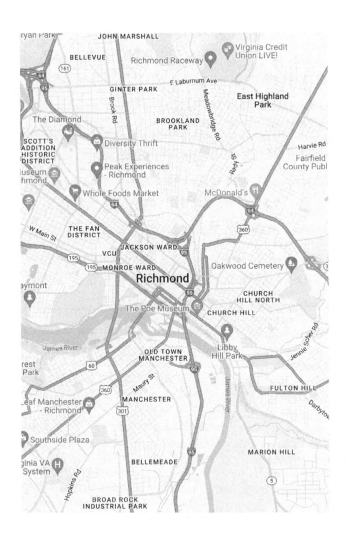

INTRODUCTION

As I sit down to pen the opening words of this Richmond Travel Guide, memories of my journey to this enchanting city come rushing back with vivid clarity. The sun-kissed cobblestone streets of Shockoe Slip, the hallowed halls of the Virginia State Capitol echoing with the footsteps of history, and the gentle embrace of the James River, all beckon me to share my tale of Richmond, a city that captured my heart and imagination.

Richmond, with its layers of history, vibrant culture, and natural splendor, is a place that defies easy description. It's a city that wears its heritage with grace, where the past harmoniously interlaces with the present, creating an intoxicating blend of tradition and innovation. Join me as I recount the highlights of my journey, a captivating odyssey that unfolded in the heart of Virginia.

Arriving in Richmond, I was greeted by the soothing sounds of the James River, a constant companion throughout my stay. It whispered tales of exploration and commerce, a lifeline that shaped Richmond's destiny. As I crossed the T. Tyler Potterfield Memorial Bridge, the river revealed its splendor, mirroring the azure sky and enveloping me in a sense of serenity.

Richmond's historic charm welcomed me with open arms as I wandered through Shockoe Slip, a district that seemed frozen in time. Cobbled pathways led me past 19th-century warehouses transformed into quaint shops and eateries. I paused at the Poe Museum, where Edgar Allan Poe's haunting words echoed through the halls, and I marveled at the mystery that clung to this literary icon.

In the heart of the city stood the magnificent Virginia State Capitol, a testament to architectural brilliance and a stage for the drama of democracy. I explored its grand chambers, envisioning the debates that shaped the nation's future. A sense of awe overcame me as I gazed at the equestrian statue of George Washington, a silent witness to history's turning points.

My culinary journey through Richmond was nothing short of delightful. At L'Opossum, I indulged in a gastronomic experience that transcended mere dining. Each dish was a work of art, a testament to the creativity of Chef David Shannon. The flavors danced on my palate, leaving a lasting impression of Richmond's culinary excellence.

As the sun dipped below the horizon, I found myself at Libby Hill Park, a vantage point that provided a breathtaking panorama of the city. The warm hues of twilight painted the skyline, and I watched as the city lights began to twinkle like stars, casting a spell that was nothing short of magical.

But Richmond's allure isn't confined to its historic precincts alone. The Lewis Ginter Botanical Garden offered a glimpse of nature's splendor, a tapestry of vibrant blooms and tranquil water features. It was a place where time slowed, and I found solace amidst the lush greenery.

Amid my exploration, I discovered the thriving art scene that defines Richmond. The Virginia Museum of Fine Arts housed a treasure trove of artistic masterpieces, from classical to contemporary. Each canvas told a story, and I found myself losing track of time amidst the brushstrokes and colors.

My journey through Richmond was marked by unforgettable moments. The Hollywood Cemetery, where American legends found their final repose, evoked a sense of reverence. The Byrd Theatre, with its classic films and opulent interiors, transported me to a bygone era of cinema. And the enchanting Maymont Estate, with its rolling gardens and friendly animal residents, charmed me with its serenity.

Before I knew it, it was time to bid adieu to this captivating city. My journey through Richmond had been nothing short of extraordinary, a tapestry of experiences that left an indelible mark on my soul. As I write these words, I hope to impart the essence of Richmond to you, the intrepid traveler ready to embark on your adventure.

So, as you leaf through the pages of this Richmond Travel Guide, I invite you to immerse yourself in the city's rich history, savor its culinary delights, and embrace its vibrant culture. Let these words be your guide as you explore Richmond, a city where every corner reveals a new story, and every moment is an opportunity to create unforgettable memories.

As you set out on your journey, remember that Richmond is more than a destination; it's an experience waiting to be embraced. So, pack your curiosity and embark on an adventure that will leave you with cherished moments and a heart full of inspiration.

Welcome to Richmond, where history, culture, and nature converge to create a tapestry of wonder and discovery.

BRIEF HISTORY

Virginia's capital, Richmond, is rich in American history and has been essential to the growth of the country from colonial days to the present. The narrative starts when English immigrants first arrived in the region at the beginning of the 17th century. William Byrd II formally laid out the city in 1737 and named it after Richmond upon Thames in England because the views of the James and Thames rivers were so similar.

During the colonial era, Richmond's advantageous position on the James River made it a major center for commerce and the expansion of Virginia's tobacco industry. In 1780, it moved from Williamsburg to become the capital of the Colony and Dominion of Virginia to better defend the state's archives from British invasion during the American Revolution.

Being the Confederate capital from 1861 to 1865, the city was a focal point throughout the Civil War. Many engagements were fought in and around Richmond during this time, leaving an enduring impression on the city. Notably, Richmond fell to Union troops in April 1865, signaling the beginning of the Confederacy's demise.

Richmond started on a path of reconstruction and development after the Civil War. The city developed into a significant industrial hub in the late 19th and early 20th centuries as a result of the construction of several factories, as well as the expansion of the banking, finance, and tobacco industries. The city was also vital to the civil rights movement, with the state capitol of Virginia serving as the focal point of several important occasions and court cases aimed at advancing equality and putting an end to segregation.

Richmond is renowned today for its rich past, which is preserved in a large number of historic structures, monuments, and museums. It's a city that offers a thriving cultural scene, a wide range of gastronomic pleasures, and outdoor activities—all while embracing its history and looking to the future. Richmond's dedication to innovation, education, and community development sets it apart as a vibrant capital city that celebrates its past while promoting progress and diversity.

GEOGRAPHY AND CLIMATE

Virginia's capital city, Richmond, is situated in a distinctive location in the Piedmont area of the state, along the James River's fall line. Due to its natural transition between the flat coastal plain to the east and the undulating hills that signal the start of the Appalachian Mountains to the west, this region has traditionally been quite important. The fall line is the actual location where navigable rivers meet the upland area. In Richmond's instance, this produced an ideal location for the city to be established since river transportation was easy to cease at this point and overland transportation was required to begin.

The geography of the city is diverse, providing both natural and urban landscapes both within its borders and in the environs. The James River is an important feature of the city's landscape, serving as a hub for current leisure, wildlife, and conservation initiatives in addition to its historical importance as a commercial route. Due to the river's proximity, the city has developed several parks and islands that are well-liked for outdoor recreation, including Belle Isle and Brown's Island.

Richmond's climate is categorized as humid subtropical, with pleasant spring and autumn seasons, warm to chilly winters, and hot and muggy summers. The city's natural charm is enhanced by the climate, which is home to a wide variety of plants and animals.

The urban design of the city is a reflection of its past growth, with older districts featuring narrow streets with grid patterns that open out into more expansive suburban regions. Richmond has a rich and diverse architectural history, with notable structures dating back to the colonial period, and the Civil War, and contemporary skyscrapers that pepper the skyline.

Richmond's proximity to major highways, railroads, and the Richmond International Airport makes it a center for travel and business in the area. Because of its advantageous position in the middle of Virginia, it serves as a crucial hub for both the cultural and economic narratives that link the country's history and geography. Eastern Seaboard.

The Greater Richmond Area, which connects Richmond to both growing suburban areas and rural landscapes, is made up of many counties around the city. Richmond's dynamic and captivating environment, which embodies a mixture of history, culture, and natural beauty unique to Virginia's capital, is made possible by the interplay of urban and natural settings inside and surrounding the city.

BEST TIME TO VISIT

The Best Months to Go

April through June is when Richmond is most beautiful. Not only will the weather be nice, but when local universities close for the summer, there won't be many people around. A visit in the autumn is especially recommended since the city is a riot of color, and spending an afternoon sipping locally crafted brews and coffees with a fall theme is a fun way to spend a day there. When the city is lit up with Christmas lights over the holidays, winter may be a pleasant time to come. Summertime visits in Virginia require overcoming other travelers and the oppressive heat.

April–June

Visit Richmond throughout the spring and early summer for the best results. The city has blooming trees and gardens, highs in the 70s and 80s, and it seems like there are festivals and activities every weekend. While the South of the James farmers market closes for the season, which spans November through April, the bustling summer session of RVA Big Market, where local merchants offer everything from baked goods to meats to jewelry to soap, gets underway. There's so much to adore about Richmond at this time of year—we could go on forever. Remember that May and June are when hotel prices start to rise, due to the combination of summer tourism and college graduation ceremonies.

Important Occurrences:

Big Market in RVA (year-round)

April is Richmond Restaurant Week.

November to April, south of the James Market

Riverrock, Dominion Energy (May)

Friday Salutations (May–June)

Juneteenth falls in June.

June–August is the Richmond Shakespeare Festival.

After Five Flowers (June-September)

July–August

In the summertime, Richmond is teeming with other travelers. Because of this, you can expect high hotel prices to correspond with the large number of visitors. A hotel should cost between $150 and $200. Additionally, you'll enjoy Virginia's hot weather, with highs that sometimes reach the low to mid-90s. These may be some of the wettest months of the year, so don't forget to bring an umbrella and some water-resistant footwear. But if you can tolerate the heat and congestion, you'll be rewarded with many chances to take part in festivals and outdoor activities.

Important Occurrences:

Big Market in RVA (year-round)

June–August is the Richmond Shakespeare Festival.

After Five Flowers (June-September)

July–August: Chesterfield County Fair

August Richmond Jazz Festival

August is the Filipino Festival.

August sees the Carytown Watermelon Festival.

September through December

The 50s to low 80s are the new normal daily temperature range for fall and early winter. Hotel prices continue to be low during the Christmas season, just rising marginally from their midsummer highs. Plan your trip for late October to see the best autumn foliage during Restaurant Week, or go in December to see the amazing Christmas lights that are displayed around the city and its neighborhoods.

January through March

Winter in Richmond is a peaceful time. If you come around this period, you won't have to deal with many people since the tourist season slows down. But be sure to dress warmly. Lows may fall into the upper 20s, while highs peak in the 50s. It's possible that there could be snow when you come, so be sure to check the weather before you go and prepare accordingly.

TRANSPORTATION

GETTING THERE

ACCESSING THE RICHMOND REGION

Via Aircraft, Rail, Car, or Large Bus

Richmond International Airport serves flights from all over the world, making the Richmond Region easily

20

accessible. All of the main airlines, including low-cost ones, provide direct flights to RIR from a large number of places. Additionally, half of all Americans live within a half-day drive of the Richmond Region. Located as we are at the intersection of I-95 and I-64, we may easily go east or west. (Hint: we're the perfect place to stop and hang out if you're on a lengthy drive up or down 95.)

You can reach here at very affordable prices via express buses. Along with three Amtrak stations—Amtrak stops at Ashland, Staples Mill, and the recently renovated Main Street terminal—we also have a sizable Greyhound terminal. Welcome, everyone.

VIA CAR

When traveling by car, getting from one end of the Richmond Region to the other is simple. It's easy to travel all around this region, from Chesterfield's Pocahontas State Park and the Metro Richmond Zoo to Kings Dominion or Ashland Train Station, and from prime retail destinations like Short Pump Town Center and Stony Point Fashion Park. There is no shortage of parking, and the area is well-connected to both ends and other locations by major roads like as I-95, which runs north and south, and I-64, which runs east and west.

VIA AIR

More than 3 million passengers pass through Richmond International Airport each year, with direct flights from major cities and connections from all around the world. Richmond's city is at a short distance from this well-designed airport, and you can travel quickly around the area by bypasses and roads.

VIA BUS OR TRAIN

Three Amtrak stations are located in the Richmond Region: the historic Main Street Station in downtown Richmond, the Amtrak station in the quaint railroad town of Ashland, and Staples Mill Road in the West End. Greyhound buses go to Richmond's core, and several express bus operators provide very cheap prices in the vicinity.

GETTING AROUND

The GRTC Pulse, walking, and bicycling are the greatest ways to travel about Richmond. The bike-share program in Richmond makes it simple to check out a bike and tour the city. You can get a close-up look at Richmond's architecture in this walking city. The city's main attractions are all within easy reach of the Pulse line of the municipal bus system. When visiting some sites, like Kings Dominion, or when you just want to give your feet a rest, a vehicle will come in useful. As an alternative, you may use a cab or rideshare to move about.

The distance between Richmond International Airport (RIC) and downtown is around ten miles southeast. To go from the airport to downtown, you may take a cab, or the bus, or hire an automobile. There are two Amtrak stations in the city as well. The Staples Mill Road Station is eight miles northwest of downtown, while the Main Street Station is situated in the city center.

Cycle

Riding a bike is a fantastic way to navigate Richmond. You can get your daily exercise in and around downtown with the dedicated bike lanes along the streets. There are 20 stations and 220 bikes in the city for RVA Bike Share. The cost of a ride is $1.75 for a 45-minute trip, but you can save money by buying a day ticket ($6) or a weekly pass ($12), which both entitle you to unlimited 45-minute rides.

On Foot

Richmond is best explored on foot, especially if you're trying to save money. With a mix of brick and paved paths, the whole city is pedestrian-friendly. Walking across the city, however, takes nearly five miles in one direction. It will be more efficient if you combine your sightseeing and take the bus or bike to the destination. Save the Virginia State Capitol, the Poe Museum, and the Virginia Holocaust Museum for another day. Instead, choose a day to explore Carytown and the Museum District, which is home to the VMFA and the Virginia Museum of History & Culture.

Automobile

Even during rush hour, Richmond traffic is manageable, which makes renting a vehicle an appealing alternative for your journey. If you choose to drive to attractions rather than bike or walk, you'll save some energy and have more flexibility to roam about the city at your own pace. However, parking may be difficult since there are three options: street parking with costs, garage parking with fees, and on-street parking with two-hour constraints. Your best bet is to park in a convenient area and spend the day exploring on foot before returning to your lodging. Having a vehicle will also help visit places outside of Richmond, such as Kings Dominion. There are a few rental companies at Richmond International Airport and throughout the city.

Cab

Richmond also offers ridesharing services like Uber and Lyft in addition to taxis. The expense of cross-city travel may quickly mount up since one-way rates can start at $12. To conserve money, use these rides seldom. The regional bus network is managed by the Greater Richmond Transit Company. The GRTC Pulse is a high-frequency line that connects Willow Lawn, which is northwest of downtown, to Rocketts Landing, which is southeast of downtown and is the finest route for visitors. Stops along this route include Shockoe Bottom, which is close to St. John's Church, and Scott's Addition, which is home to many of the city's breweries. Daily, from 5 or 6 a.m., pulse buses operate about every 10 to 15 minutes. up until 11:30 p.m. and begin running at 11:30 p.m. every 30 minutes. until one in the morning. One-way fares are $1.50. The standard GRTC routes tend to serve regions that are further distant from the major landmarks and operate less often than the Pulse lines.

ACCOMMODATION

LUXURY HOTELS

The Jefferson Hotel

The Jefferson Hotel in Richmond, Virginia, which opened its doors to visitors in 1895, has won several awards. Travel experts agree with what actual customers have said, namely that the hotel's décor, furniture, and personnel all ooze Southern charm. The large rooms are highly praised by recent guests and provide luxurious amenities including Nespresso coffee machines, Molton Brown bath products, and personalized bedding. Reserve one of the Ginter Suites for an additional dose of luxury. Spanning more than 1,000 square feet, these rooms have a kitchenette, a dressing area, and a king-sized bed, among other amenities. The indoor pool and private outdoor sundeck of this downtown hotel are among the most popular features. Prior guests also commend the on-site eatery Lemaire. Upscale restaurant Lemaire serves modern American cuisine. The Jefferson Hotel's additional bonus is its convenient location, which makes it easy to explore the city's Museum District and the Virginia State Capitol.

The Hotel Berkeley

Situated in the Shockoe Slip neighborhood of downtown Richmond, The Berkeley Hotel offers convenient access to well-known landmarks such as the Virginia State Capitol and the Capitol Square monuments. The Edgar Allan Poe Museum and other locations are only a short drive away. The Berkeley Hotel welcomes visitors with chic guest rooms with high ceilings, cherry wood furnishings, and contemporary amenities like free Wi-Fi, coffee machines, and terry bathrobes. Although the hotel's helpful personnel and historical charm are praised by recent guests, they do comment that the rooms may need some updating. Visitors also give the Dining Room a thumbs up for its classy atmosphere and delicious appetizers, which include Southern favorites.

Short Pump's Hilton Richmond Hotel & Spa

This Hilton has a knack for making visitors feel very at ease. Regular guests say they feel cared for by the personnel on the resort in a manner that few other hotels have managed to replicate. Furthermore, rooms are often praised as being both pleasant and spotless. The Hilton Richmond offers free Wi-Fi, workstations with ergonomic seats, and 42-inch flat-screen HDTVs as standard amenities. Other handy on-site services that get great reviews from visitors include the delicious Shula's Steakhouse (a guest favorite) and Aroma Cafe, which serves Starbucks coffee. The Aura Spa & Salon, a fitness facility, and a swimming pool are all located on the premises. Furthermore, the Hilton Richmond is just east of the Short Pump Town Center. Although the hotel is situated around 15 miles northwest of Richmond's city center, this is a disadvantage, visitors had little to no complaints about the commute. Moreover, guests who stay here may accrue and spend Hilton Honors points, thanks to the hotel's affiliation with Hilton.

Richmond's Quirk Hotel

Recent visitors to Richmond, Virginia's boutique Quirk Hotel say that the hip atmosphere of the establishment is one of its greatest features. Recent guests have praised the hotel, which is situated along Broad Street among the downtown arts and design area, as eccentric—in a good way—with a sleek design and thoughtful detailing. Natural light floods the guest rooms, which also have hardwood flooring, original furniture, artwork from the area, minibars, coffee machines, and free Wi-Fi. Travelers are free to follow their hobbies, such as working out at the on-site fitness facility or looking at the Quirk Art Gallery's rotating exhibitions. Once you're hungry, try the seasonal, locally produced food at Maple & Pine restaurant, which has received positive reviews from previous patrons despite being a touch pricey. While most guests had a positive overall experience, a few expressed dissatisfaction with the level of service and accommodations compared to what they would have expected from a high-end, boutique hotel.

BUDGET HOTELS

The Hostel HI Richmond

Cost: The starting price for a bed in a shared dorm is around $30 per night.

Location: Right in the middle of Richmond's downtown, it's a great starting point for foot exploration of the area.

Overview: HI Richmond Hostel offers modest, clean lodging with a community vibe, making it the perfect choice for single travelers and those on a limited budget. There is a sitting space, a community kitchen, and shared bathrooms. For those who want more solitude, there are also private rooms accessible. The hostel is a great place to meet other visitors because of its convenient location and welcoming attitude.

The Richmond South Red Roof Inn

Price: Nightly prices start at around $70.00.

Location: This motel is conveniently along I-95 and just a short drive from the Virginia State Capitol and downtown Richmond.

Overview: For those arriving by vehicle, the Red Roof Inn is a nice option since it provides simple lodging and free parking. There is free WiFi, a flat-screen TV, and a work desk in each room. Additionally, some rooms include mini-fridges and microwaves. Pets are welcome at the hotel, and there is no additional fee for customers to stay with their animal companions.

Wyndham Richmond Midlothian Turnpike's Super 8

Cost: The starting rate is around $65 per night.

Location: This hotel is conveniently close to Richmond's Southside and Chesterfield Towne Center, all of which are accessible via the Midlothian Turnpike.

Overview: This Super 8 provides affordable prices along with essential amenities including parking, free Wi-Fi, and breakfast. Microwaves, refrigerators, and cable TV are provided in the rooms. For visitors who are in the Midlothian region or who need to get to Richmond's southside attractions quickly, the hotel's location is handy. For tourists who prioritize location and money, it's a simple, no-frills alternative.

UNIQUE STAYS

Cost: Nightly rates begin at around $150.

Location: Many of Richmond's restaurants, shops, and museums are easily accessible by foot from our quaint B&B, which is located in the city's historic Fan District.

Overview: Dubbed "The One," this bed and breakfast provides distinctively furnished rooms that combine contemporary conveniences with classic charm.

Luxurious linen, free Wi-Fi, and private bathrooms are amenities included in every accommodation. There is a gorgeous garden, a comfortable common room, and a superb breakfast offered every morning for guests to enjoy. It's the ideal option for anybody searching for a home away from home because of its cozy and welcoming ambiance.

Linden Row Hotel

Price: Nightly prices start at around $120.

Location: This hotel is adjacent to the Greater Richmond Convention Center and the Virginia State Capitol, situated in the center of Richmond's downtown.

Overview: Offering visitors a taste of Southern charm and warmth, the Linden Row Inn is a boutique historic inn. The inn is made up of seven-row homes that were built in the middle of the 1800s and exquisitely refurbished to provide cozy, contemporary lodging while maintaining its historical relevance. Free Wi-Fi, in-room spa treatments upon request, and a free shuttle to downtown locations are among the amenities. A peaceful haven from the bustle of the city is its beautiful courtyard.

ATTRACTIONS AND ACTIVITIES

HISTORIC SITES AND MUSEUMS

The Virginia Museum of Fine Arts

When comparing the Virginia Museum of Fine Arts holdings to those of art museums in considerably bigger cities, the majority of visitors are pleased.

Notable for its five exquisite Fabergé eggs, this Museum District gem also has extensive collections of African, Indian, and Tibetan art, as well as pieces by Cézanne, Renoir, and Degas. Particularly striking to recent visitors was the McGlothlin Collection of American Art. The VMFA often hosts several temporary exhibitions that cover a wide range of topics, including Asian religions, jewelry, Black life in Virginia, and more, in addition to its permanent collections.

Tip: advise allocating at least several hours to browse since it's hard to see everything in a single visit. Whenever possible, try to visit many times while in Richmond. You'll want more time to explore the grounds and the sculpture garden at the museum in addition to the time needed to see all of the exhibits inside. Along with the incredible collections, visitors were also taken aback by the on-site Amuse Restaurant, which is often ranked among Richmond's greatest dining establishments.

The museum lies around 4 miles west of Richmond's city center. At 10 a.m., the VMFA is open. every day. The museum closes at five o'clock on Saturdays through Tuesdays; the galleries and store are open until nine o'clock on Wednesday, Thursday, and Friday. While general entry is always free, tickets may be needed for some events and special exhibitions. It will cost you $6 to park. The GRTC Pulse bus route serves the neighborhood if you'd prefer not to pay the charge.

State Capitol of Virginia

After Virginia withdrew from the Union in 1861, Richmond was designated as the Confederacy's capital. The General Assembly of the state and the Confederate Congress thereafter met at the city's capital building. These days, tourists come to this massive structure to learn about the history of the Virginia government as well as to take pictures of its architecture, which was partly created by French architect Charles-Louis Clérisseau and Thomas Jefferson. Capitol Square, the surrounding neighborhood, is home to various monuments honoring notable Virginians including George Washington and Edgar Allan Poe, as well as the civil rights struggle.

Recent visitors reported being pleasantly pleased by the level of interest they found during their visit to the capital building. Reviewers commended the informed guides in addition to the distinctive architecture and urged future tourists to take advantage of the free guided tour.

The public may visit the capital starting at 9 a.m. on Monday through Saturday. until 5:00 p.m. Sunday from 1 to 5 p.m. as well. Free guided tours last one hour and start at 10 a.m. until 4 p.m. From Monday to Saturday. Free guided tours are offered on Sundays from 1 to 4 p.m.

Museum of History and Culture in Virginia

428 N Boulevard is the address.

The Virginia Historical Society is in charge of running the Virginia Museum of History & Culture. The goal of the organization is to use inclusive storytelling to showcase Virginia's history in its totality. You'll notice that the building achieves that goal as soon as you enter it. The museum is home to a vast collection of historic objects from the commonwealth, including tools, maps, photos, letters, and artwork. "The Story of Virginia," the major exhibit, traces the history of Virginia from the time of the Native American tribes that lived there thousands of years ago to the colonist invasion to the present. Other displays use paintings to examine the commonwealth's history with weaponry and the state of Virginia. Do you want to conduct your research? Visit the on-site library to check into historical documents and start your family history research.

This museum has received great reviews from recent visitors, who called it an entertaining and instructive rainy-day pastime. Even though the Virginia Museum of Fine Arts is just next door, many claim you can't complete both in a single day. To thoroughly explore both, you will need to set up a day for each.

Holocaust Museum in Virginia

2000 E. is the address. Cary Street.

In addition to having a wealth of Civil War history, Richmond is home to an amazing and poignant Holocaust museum. The Virginia Holocaust Museum was established in 1997 by Jay Ipson, one of the youngest Holocaust survivors from Richmond. It tells two stories: a comprehensive account of the Holocaust's significance in world history and the experience and survival of the Ipson family. Both the Ipson family's trip and the accounts of survivors who resettled in Richmond will be told to visitors.

Several recent visitors praised this organization highly, citing its poignant and beautiful displays as one of the top Holocaust museums in the country.

Virginia's Black History Museum & Cultural Center

The address is 122 W. Leigh Street.

Previous visitors have described the Black History Museum & Cultural Center of Virginia as a wonderful treasure. The way the material is presented, which combines interactive touch screens with conventional methods like artifacts and placards, was very well-liked by visitors to the museum. With a focus on Black Virginians specifically, the exhibitions recount the history of Black Americans. Monthly activities and temporary speciality exhibitions, such as a 2020 show that presented the narrative of enslaved peoples at Monticello, are held at the museum in addition to permanent exhibits.

The museum is located in the Jackson Ward neighborhood's historic Leigh Street Armory. Adult admission is $10, student and senior admission is $8, and children 4 to 12 years old are $6. Younger than 4 are admitted free of charge. BHMVA's hours have been restricted to 10 a.m. from Thursday through Saturday because of the coronavirus epidemic. until 5:00 p.m.

Virginia Science Museum

2500 W is the address. Wide St.

Former visitors, both young and old at heart, have nothing but praise for the Science Museum of Virginia. The interactive features throughout the place were liked by kids and parents. Visitors without children said that the museum's offerings were appropriate for adults as well, pointing out that nothing felt too juvenile.

This place has a variety of exhibits on various subjects, such as time and motion, mental and physical health, and a light show for kids under five. Several shifting exhibits are also present. One exhibit from 2021, for instance, focused on mental disorders. Throughout the facility, there are many "Experiences" to enhance your stay. Historians may see a performance of astronaut Sally Ride's life, while aspiring scientists can construct their gaming controller. (Note: Some "Experiences" are age-specific, while others are appropriate for all children.) If you're looking for more interactive fun, sign up for a class at The Forge to create things like mechanical hand or nail art and string art.

The Museum of the American Civil War

480 Tredegar St. is the address.

The American Civil War Museum is housed in three locations: the White House of the Confederacy and the American Civil War Museum at Historic Tredegar in Richmond, Virginia; the Museum of the

Confederacy-Appomattox is located in Appomattox, Virginia, about 95 miles west of Richmond. Civil War enthusiasts must visit this museum because of its extensive collection of Confederate relics, guns, and other items.

"A People's Contest: Struggles for Nation and Freedom in Civil War America," a permanent exhibit at Historic Tredegar, examines the Civil War chronologically from the perspectives of both citizens and military commanders. Visitors give the multimedia show excellent praise. Confederate President Jefferson Davis formerly resided at the White House of the Confederacy, which is located close to Tredegar. All day long, guided tours of the home depart from the foyer of the museum. Visitors to the museum in the past have praised the knowledgeable docents and the well-preserved house. "Enacting Freedom: Black Virginians in the Age of Emancipation," an exhibit that examines Black Virginians' experiences after independence from slavery, may be found in Appomattox if you want to go further.

PARKS AND OUTDOOR ACTIVITIES

ARCPARK

All ages and abilities are welcome to play and work out together at the 2.4-acre gorgeous and entertaining ARCpark. Ample swings, including an adult-sized changing table and an extra-wide ramp leading to a wheelchair-accessible treehouse with a four-ton, repurposed eucalyptus stump; a specially constructed multisensory wall with panels that stimulate touch, hearing, and sight; a play house, a small stage, water troughs, and music instruments for creative play; handicap-accessible fitness equipment and a multipurpose playing court; water misting stations; a large, shaded pavilion with nine picnic tables; a family restroom with an adult-sized changing table; and charging stations for electric wheelchairs are among the special features.

Saunders Avenue, 3600

Richmond, Virginia 23227

Belle Isle

Belle Isle, which is a part of the James River Park System, is primarily accessible via footbridge for pedestrians from Tredegar St. on the north bank. Another way to get there is via rock-hopping from the south shore or over a wooden bridge close to 22nd St. Though the broad, level rocks that encircle the island are excellent for tanning, swimming is not advised because of the strong Hollywood Rapids. Youngsters need to be watched after. A granite wall for rock climbing, wheelchair-accessible fishing at the quarry pond, interpretive historical sites, woodland walks, and mountain bike routes are additional amenities.

PARK BENSLEY

A picnic area, playgrounds, tennis courts, ball fields, and walking paths are just a few of the recreational features that this 17-acre park has to offer. Within the park, the Bensley Community Building offers a range of activities and events for elders, adults, and young people.

Drewry's Bluff Road, 2900

23237 North Chesterfield, Virginia

(804) 748-1623

OUTDOOR ACTIVITIES

Enjoy the freedom of the great outdoors when you visit Richmond, Virginia. Take a stroll along the James River's rushing Pipeline or take in the stunning views from the new T. Pott Bridge. Take in the paintings and historic landmarks while strolling along the Canal Walk. There are several beautiful parks and bike and pet-friendly routes across the city. You can discover entertaining Richmond attractions and activities whether you're organizing a romantic weekend vacation or a family outing. Here are a few of Richmond, Virginia's best outdoor activities.

James River

The James River has a 10,000 square-mile watershed and flows 430 miles through the center of Virginia, from the Blue Ridge Mountains to the Chesapeake Bay. Activities available include rafting, tubing, kayaking, and paddleboarding. The James River Association connects people to Virginia's greatest natural resource while acting as a custodian and advocate for the river. The James River Park System, a network of hiking paths, provides lovely river vistas as well.

Go to Maymont

Richmond, Virginia's Maymont is a 100-acre public park and Victorian home. It includes Children's Farm, a nature center, formal gardens, an arboretum, a carriage collection, native animal displays, and Maymont Mansion, which is now a historic house museum. Visitors may also explore the several hiking paths on the site or take guided nature hikes. Maymont was recognized by the American Planning Association as one of the top 10 public places in 2011.

The Virginia Capital Trail

The Virginia Capital Trail is a 51.7-mile paved bike and pedestrian route that connects Jamestown and Richmond, Virginia, spanning four counties. The first and current capitals of the Colony of Virginia may be reached by foot or by bicycle; Williamsburg, the last colonial capital, serves as a backup destination. Gorgeous views of the James River and the surrounding landscape may be seen from the route.

Ride on a Hot Air Balloon

Hot air balloon rides provide visitors with an aerial perspective of Richmond's breathtaking landscape. A hot air balloon flight is the ideal way to observe

Richmond's stunning city from above. Your trip in a hot air balloon will leave you with lifelong memories. Your hot air balloon floats above the peaceful, scenic scenery in soft winds. For a group of friends or a solitary trip, you may hire out a balloon.

ART GALLERIES

1. The Museum of Fine Arts, Virginia (VMFA)

200 N. is the location. Boulevard Arthur Ashe, Richmond, Virginia

Cost: Free general entry; tickets may need to be paid for special exhibits.

A premier organization that is notable both in Richmond and internationally is the Virginia Museum of Fine Arts. More than 33,000 pieces of art spanning 5,000 years of global history are part of its vast collection. Art from Africa to East Asia, America to Europe, and beyond is available at the VMFA. There's always something new to discover thanks to the museum's shifting displays. The VMFA offers studio art courses, special events, and educational activities in addition to its stunning galleries. The Sculpture Garden, which is open for longer hours, provides a calm environment where art and nature harmoniously coexist.

2. 1708 Gallery

319 W is the location. Richmond, Virginia's Broad Street

Open from 11 a.m. on Tuesday through Friday. – 5 p.m.; 11 a.m. on Saturday. 4 p.m.

Cost: There is no admission fee.

The non-profit 1708 Gallery presents outstanding new works of art by well-known and up-and-coming creators. Recognized for its dedication to avant-garde displays and events, the 1708 Gallery serves as a forum for modern art that addresses social, political, and cultural concerns. The gallery is a vibrant place that promotes conversation between artists and the community since it often provides artists lectures, workshops, and performances that go along with their shows. Its central position in Richmond's thriving art area and dedication to accessibility make it an accessible place for everyone to see cutting-edge contemporary art.

3. The Odd Gallery

Address: 207 W. Richmond, Virginia's Broad Street

Open from 10 a.m. on Monday through Saturday. – 6 p.m.; 11 a.m. on Sunday. – 5 p.m.

Cost: There is no admission fee.

Quirk Gallery is distinguished by its distinct approach to art, combining great art exhibits with handcrafted products. Situated in the center of Richmond's downtown, Quirk is a beautifully restored historic building that showcases artwork from both domestic and international artists. A boutique hotel and a store where guests may buy unique crafts, jewelry, and artwork complement the gallery area. The carefully chosen shows at Quirk often include the work of up-and-coming artists in addition to more well-known ones. If you want to get a sense of Richmond's creative scene and maybe even bring home a piece of art that inspires you, this gallery is a must-see.

FAMILY-FRIENDLY ATTRACTIONS

1. Maymont

Location: Richmond, VA 23220, 1700 Hampton St.

Maymont is a 100-acre estate that offers families the ideal outdoor adventure and discovery for a day. Explore the lovely gardens, pay a visit to the Maymont Mansion, and take the kids to the Nature Center to learn about Virginia's fauna and get up close and personal with animals. Savor strolling routes, picnics, and seasonal activities like the Cherry Blossom Festival at the Japanese Garden.

Garden at Lewis Ginter Botanical

1800 Lakeside Ave. Richmond, VA 23228 is the address.

Family-friendly activities and a verdant haven of natural beauty may be found at the Lewis Ginter Botanical Garden. See themed gardens, such as a treehouse and water play areas at the Children's Garden. This garden is a year-round family attraction thanks to seasonal activities like the Dominion Energy GardenFest of Lights around the holidays.

King Dominion

Head to Kings Dominion, which is approximately 25 miles north of Richmond, when you and your children need a vacation from all the historical lessons the city has to offer. Recent visitors applaud this 400-acre water and entertainment park for its family-friendly activities and reasonable size. All of the roller coasters here were very popular with thrill-seekers, with the wooden Grizzly coaster drawing them through a thick forest being a particular favorite. An additional benefit is that the standard entrance price covers access to the family-friendly Soak City water park.

Recent guests had just one grievance, and that was over the expensive cuisine. There are a few covered picnic sites in the visitor parking lot if you would want to pack food or beverages to eat before entering the park, even though you are not allowed to bring outside food or beverages inside the park. If you want to purchase water or soft drinks inside the park, you may want to think about getting the commemorative bottle. Even though it costs $13.99, you'll get free refills all day long.

Doswell, Virginia is home to Kings Dominion, which is around a 30-minute drive north of Richmond's city center. From Memorial Day weekend through Labor Day weekend, the majority of the facilities are open daily beginning at 11 a.m. up to 7:00 p.m. Every day at lunchtime, the Soak City park closes at six or seven o'clock p.m. Additionally, Kings Dominion is open on certain weekends in early May, on a few days in April, and on weekends in October. Online purchases of general entry for adults and children run $55 per person. You would have to pay over $66 per person if you wait to get your tickets at the entrance.

SHOPPING

Clementine

Clementine is an upscale consignment store that focuses on offering women's designer and modern clothing options. Every item at the shop, which has been open for more than 15 years, has been hand-selected for quality and elegance.

Richmond, Virginia 23221, USA 3118 W Cary St

Ledbury

Ledbury is a men's apparel retailer dedicated to premium, cutting-edge styles that is based in Richmond, Virginia. The business offers a wide selection of clothes for every occasion and produces its items in tiny European workshops and Italian textile mills.

23220 USA, Richmond, VA 315 W Broad St.

Mod & Soul

Mod&Soul offers a unique selection of fashionable women's apparel from American-made, limited-edition businesses. The business offers a unique shopping experience at any time of the month since it takes part in Richmond's First Fridays Art Walk. The store's homemade fixtures constructed of repurposed wood and industrial pipes add to its adorable boho vibe.

23220 USA, Richmond, VA 323 W Broad St.

Fashion Park at Stony Point

The Stony Point Fashion Park is an outdoor shopping center including upscale stores, a movie theater, and a refined, traditional atmosphere. The complex has plenty of parking as well as a food court with plenty of vendors selling snacks and beverages. The mall has lovely fountains, interesting outdoor entertainment, and a park-like ambience.

Stony Point Parkway, 9200, Richmond, Virginia 23235, USA

NIGHTLIFE AND ENTERTAINMENT

Virginia's capitol is all business throughout the day. However, this elegant seat of commonwealth authority is poised to let loose at night.

Richmond's taverns, theaters, and clubs provide something for every taste, whether it is classical theater or simply a pour of your favorite poison.

Drinking in Richmond ranges from sophisticated wine bars to dive pubs that are well-known for their affordable beers and unique local flair. One favorite place to go is Wonderland's "drunken circus," a vibrant punk-pop culture enclave owned by an ex-wrestler where everyone knows your name (or will by the end of the night). Visit Saison, a quaint speakeasy-style pub, for inventive drinks and excellent bar bites. If you're searching for a less formal evening that's nevertheless a step up from the typical diving experience, Heritage is the place to go.

Live Band Performances

Would you rather unwind to some acoustic folk music or spice up your evening with some funk? There's a jam for you in Richmond's music scene. Every night of the week, there's always something going on at The Camel, ranging from unpolished performances by local singers to well-known bands covering a broad spectrum of genres. Poe's Pub has live blues, zydeco, rock, and country music. This neighborhood tavern serves delicious food, a cold pint, and an intriguing ambiance. If you're searching for even larger bands, check out what's on at The National, a musical space converted from a historic theater that features performers that might be considered for the Grammy Awards.

Dance Floor Motions

Enter one of the numerous dancing clubs in Richmond if sitting still is the last thing you want to do after the day is done. Godfrey's is a well-liked destination for club-goers who appreciate a nice mix from the D.J. and an enticing drink special. It is recognized for its trendy attitude, unique lighting effects, varied audience, and engaging drag acts. The Tobacco Company Club is as well-known for its live music and dancing floor in the first-floor bar as it is for its elaborate, classic design, dress code, and prime rib.

An evening of fine arts

Richmond has a fantastic theatrical scene if you'd rather take in the local artistic culture above anything else. The Virginia Repertory Theatre presents world-class plays and beloved musicals for a broad audience. You may have a great time laughing all night long at the Coalition Theater thanks to their hilarious improv sessions. Apart from other smaller theater groups operating in the area, you may see the Richmond Ballet in action or attend exclusive events like music, movies, or cultural exhibits at the esteemed Virginia Museum of Fine Arts.

DINING AND CUISINE

SOUTHERN CUISINE

Dining Astute foodies are well aware of Richmond. However, it's understandable why many visitors come to Richmond with low expectations given that nearby culinary hotspots like Charleston, South Carolina, and Washington, D.C., often overshadow Virginia's capital. But when they get there, they discover a metropolis full of both foreign and American food.

The Black population in Richmond has left a lasting impression on the city's food culture. Named after the much-loved Richmond resident and food enthusiast Mr Croaker, Croaker's Spot is a local institution that serves up substantial seafood servings that are adored by both residents and tourists. Two other favorites for soul cuisine and Southern cookery are Jackie's Restaurant and Shrimps. Another favorite is the Ethiopian eatery, Addis. It is highly praised for its genuine food as well as its array of vegetarian alternatives. Consuming no gluten at all? Drop by 521 Waffles & Biscuits. The restaurant serves delicious gluten-free waffles and biscuits to its customers. Visit BLK RVA's eating page to get a complete list of Black-owned eateries. If you're planning a trip in March, don't miss Richmond's Black Restaurant Experience, where you can sample cuisine prepared by some of the top Black chefs in the region, see culinary demos, and take part in other food-related activities.

Some more places you just must see are Rappahannock (taste the oysters from the Chesapeake Bay), Heritage (gorge on the pig fries), and The Roosevelt (share the pork rind nachos, please). Usually held in April and October, the city's biennial restaurant week offers discounts on meals at some of the greatest restaurants in town.

TOP RESTAURANTS

Lehja.

This contemporary Indian gem is located in Short Pump Towne Center, an outdoor mall in Richmond, and it has an incredible wine selection from the master of hospitality Sandjeep "Sunny" Baweja. Lehja's menu features creative dishes like stuffed paneer tikka and shrimp chicken zafrani, as well as traditional regional fare like seafood Kerala curry and perfectly seasoned biryani.

Suite 910, 11800 W Broad St., Richmond, VA 23233

Brenner Pass, a contemporary, large restaurant designed by Top Chef finalist Brittanny Anderson as a tribute to the cuisine and wine of the Alps, serves dishes including dry-aged cote de boeuf au poivre, potato-topped flammkuchen, and fondue in Dansk pots. However, be sure to save space for a visit to Black Lodge, the lively dive bar that was founded during the epidemic. There, killer cocktails go well with the "Tower of Power," which is an assortment of hot dogs, patty melts, and French fries that instantly fulfil late-night desires. Are you looking for something a little bit more German? Visit The Metzger, a sibling restaurant in Church Hill, for an unparalleled brunch experience, including the Frühstück Brett (charcuterie, pretzel roll, and soft egg).

Richmond, Virginia 23230; 3200 Rockbridge St., #100

Texas Craft Barbeque by ZZQ

Known for having some of the greatest barbecues in Richmond, this Texas-style barbecue restaurant blends smoke into a variety of tender, meaty dishes that are served on a first-come, first-served basis beginning at 11 a.m. Stock the tray high with marbled brisket, enormous beef ribs, and pulled pork shoulder. Special weekly treks are worth it for Sunday-only bacon ribs and handmade pastrami available only on Fridays. Try the pound of pastrami or eat it as a sandwich with "giddy-up" sauce and handmade kraut. Eazzy Burger, the team's more recent burger joint next door, is a partnership with nearby Ardent Craft Ales.
Richmond, Virginia 23230, 3201 W Moore St., (804) 528-5648

Stella's

Stella's, a warm Greek neighborhood restaurant owned by the Giavos family, greets you with the aroma of garlic and oregano even before you enter the door.

Stock the table with flaming mushroom saganaki, flaky tiropita, and keftedes (lamb and beef meatballs), and get ready to share. Moussaka (creamy artichoke dip) and roasted lamb over butter noodles are two examples of generously portioned Greek comfort cuisine. Look out for the six Stella's Grocery outlets across the town; these are markets that specialize in gourmet goods and pre-made meals, each with a little something extra.

(804) 358-2011, 1012 Lafayette St., Richmond, VA 23221

Garnett's

Some of the tastiest sandwiches in the city are served at this laid-back, cozy corner eatery. Try one of the several "Croques," such as the original Scuffletown Chicken Sandwich, which has large pieces of chicken with a pickle twang, or the Croque Park Avenue, which has black forest ham, gruyere, spinach, and garlic aioli covered in a layer of mornay sauce. Two of Richmond's best-kept secrets are Garnett's happy hour ($3 glasses of wine and pints of beer, 4 to 6 p.m.) and its weeklong $33 date night deal (any two menu items plus a bottle of wine or pitcher of beer after 6 p.m.).

(804) 367-7909, 2001 Park Ave., Richmond, VA 23220

CULTURAL INSIGHTS AND EVENTS

ANNUAL FESTIVALS AND EVENTS

Events Shamrock The Block (March to mid-April)

Shamrock the Block, Richmond's first event, is held on the weekend closest to St. Patrick's Day on the Boulevard between Leigh Street and Broad Street (near the rowdy Scott's Addition area).

This free celebration features food, drinks, and music—all the classic festival fare, with everyone dressed in green and eager to bid winter farewell and welcome better weather. However, admission is not free, so that would be lovely.

Late March French Film Festival

Though it is unlike anything else happening in Richmond, Virginia, the French Film Festival is included in our list of events in Richmond because of its growing popularity in both the United States and France.

The previous French Ambassador to the U.S. even labeled it the most significant French film festival in the nation (are there that many?).

For more than 25 years, the "festival" has allowed some 1,000 filmmakers, screenwriters, actors, and other artists to share their work with a wider audience. The historic Byrd Theatre in Carytown, Richmond, is the venue for all of the film screenings.

Aside: be sure to check to see a newly released film at the Byrd Theatre for only $4 when it's not the French Film Festival.

March's Late Irish Festival

This more traditional Irish event, which is often celebrated the week following St. Patrick's Day, begins with a march of bagpipers dressed in kilts.

Situated on the historic Church Hill, the Irish Festival is probably more family-friendly and less boisterous than Shamrock the Block.

Festival de Cuisine Lebanese (mid-May)

Held in St. Anthony's Maronite Catholic Church, this event has been named the best festival in the area—which is noteworthy given all the festivals Richmond has, which is why this site was created. The Lebanese Food Festival is celebrating its 35th year in 2019, so they're doing something right!

Riverrock Dominion (Mid-May)

Every year, over 100,000 people visit Brown's Island and Historic Tredegar for Riverrock, which is reputed to be the biggest and best outdoor sports and music event in the United States.

Take a look at this quotation from their website to get an idea of why this Richmond event draws so many attendees: "From music to mud pits, motorcycles to beer, SUPs to pooches, and climbing to kayaking - it's distinctly RVA! become down and dirty with us, watch the audience become enthralled by professional athletes, and rock the day and night away.

That, in my opinion, pretty well covers everything! An exceptional occasion featuring activities to occupy and/or amuse everyone. You won't want to miss Richmond's next event!

MUSIC AND THEATER

Live Music: Richmond's music culture is varied and inclusive, appealing to a broad spectrum of preferences. You may discover all genres of music in the city, including jazz, blues, rock, hip-hop, and indie. Numerous venues often host local performers and traveling bands on their stages. Live music venues that are well-liked include:

The National: Both well-known and up-and-coming performers perform at this historic theater in Richmond's downtown. Music lovers like it for its magnificent interior and superb sound.

The Broadberry is a vibrant music venue that hosts both national and local bands. It is located in the Fan District of the city. Artists and their listeners can form a personal bond in this intimate setting.

Friday Salutations: In the spring and early summer, Brown's Island hosts this weekly music series. This is a great chance to take in live music outside by the picturesque James River.

Theater: Richmond has a thriving theater industry that has a variety of venues showcasing anything from modern dramas and musicals to historic plays. These are some noteworthy theaters:

Virginia Repertory Theatre: renowned for its excellent presentations, this theater presents a range of plays, including both original and Broadway blockbusters. Venues like the November Theatre and the Children's Theatre at Willow Lawn host their shows. The Swift Creek Mill Theatre, which is a short drive outside of Richmond, is well-known for both its varied schedule of plays and musicals and its historic appeal. If you want a more personal theatrical experience, this is a great option.

Intimate theater in the Arts District Firehouse Theatre presents provocative, avant-garde shows. It often features an experimental theater and creative works.

Through festivals and events like the Acts of Faith Festival and the Richmond Folk Festival, which showcase the city's dedication to creative expression and cultural diversity, Richmond also honors its performing arts community.

LOCAL CUSTOMS AND TRADITIONS

Southern Hospitality: The friendly and inviting ambiance of Richmond is well-known. Making guests feel at home is a deeply embedded tradition of Southern hospitality, and residents take great delight in it. It's customary to say "hello" to strangers and start a discussion with neighbours.

Richmond's culinary scene: Richmonders place a high value on food and have a few peculiar eating habits. Savouring traditional Southern fare like fried chicken, collard greens, and biscuits—often paired with sweet tea or craft beer—is one of the most treasured customs. Barbecue is another great interest of many Richmonders, and enthusiasts of various barbecue styles, from tomato-based to vinegar-based sauces, enjoy a friendly competition.

Historical Heritage: A significant part of Richmond's character is its past as the Confederacy's capitol. Locals take great satisfaction in using monuments, museums, and yearly celebrations to preserve and honor this past. There is much thought and debate around the Emancipation Proclamation and the Civil War.

Outdoor Activities: Richmonders have a deep passion for the great outdoors and a long heritage of appreciating the area's natural beauty. Locals like the James River as a meeting spot because of its beautiful parks and aquatic sports like tubing and kayaking. For many, hiking in the neighboring Blue Ridge Mountains is another treasured custom.

Music & Arts: Local musicians, artists, and cultural events are traditionally supported in Richmond, which has a strong arts scene. Throughout the year, the city offers some live music festivals, art exhibits, and concerts. One popular event that unites the community for live music is the Friday Cheers outdoor concert series.

Engagement with the Community: Richmond has a long history of volunteering and community participation. Numerous citizens actively participate in local groups, charitable organizations, and projects that enhance the city. The local culture has a strong emphasis on civic duty and a feeling of community.

Seasonal Celebrations: Richmond takes great pride in marking the arrival of each new season. Pumpkin fields, apple picking, and tours of the vibrant foliage herald fall. Winter brings with it the customs of the holidays, such as parades and bright light displays. Summer is all about outdoor events, grilling, and water sports, while spring brings cherry blossoms, garden tours, and outdoor markets.

DAY TRIPS AND EXCURSIONS

NEARBY HISTORICAL TOWNS

Williamsburg: An Exploration into Colonial Times

Williamsburg is a living history museum that takes tourists back to the American colonial period and is just a short drive from Richmond. The Williamsburg

Historic Area is a painstakingly recreated 18th-century village that has interactive displays, historic buildings, and costumed interpreters. In addition to seeing the Governor's Palace and Duke of Gloucester Street, tourists may take in everyday life reenactments from the colonial era. It's the ideal vacation spot for both families and history buffs.

Charlottesville: A Tour of the University of Virginia and Monticello

About an hour's drive from Richmond, Charlottesville provides a unique combination of natural beauty, history, and culture. Discover more about the lives of one of America's Founding Fathers by seeing the exquisitely built estate at Monticello, the former home of Thomas Jefferson. Furthermore, the Jefferson-designed University of Virginia campus is a UNESCO World Heritage site that is well worth a visit. Stroll around The Lawn and investigate the ancient Rotunda.

Petersburg: Discover the Past of the Civil War

Petersburg, which is just a short distance south of Richmond, was crucial to the American Civil War.

History buffs may learn about the Siege of Petersburg, a protracted and significant battle of the war, by touring the Petersburg National Battlefield. In addition, the city has a quaint old quarter with museums, a thriving artistic scene, and well-preserved architecture.

A Charming Town with Victorian Traits is Staunton. Staunton, which is tucked away in the Shenandoah Valley, is renowned for its Victorian-era buildings and rich cultural legacy. Many old structures can be found in the town's downtown, one of which is the exquisitely renovated Stonewall Jackson Hotel. Don't pass up the chance to see the Blackfriars Playhouse, home of the American Shakespeare Center, in Staunton for a Shakespearean experience.

NATURAL WONDERS AND STATE PARKS

Shenandoah National Park, only a few hours' drive from Richmond, provides an unrivaled chance to be in touch with nature. A 105-mile scenic byway called

Skyline Drive winds through the park, offering stunning vistas of the Blue Ridge Mountains, verdant woods, and tumbling waterfalls. Wildlife aficionados may see deer, black bears, and a wide diversity of bird species. Hiking enthusiasts may explore several paths, ranging from short walks to demanding excursions.

Park Natural Bridge: An Amazing Geological Wonder

One of Virginia's most famous natural marvels is located at Natural Bridge State Park, about two hours drive from Richmond. For generations, people have been enthralled by the 215-foot-tall limestone arch known as the Natural Bridge. Discover the geological and historical importance of this magnificent creation by strolling along the walking paths, stopping by the Monacan Indian Living History exhibit, and going on a guided tour.

A Wonderland of Wetlands: The Great Dismal Swamp National Wildlife Refuge

The Great Dismal Swamp National Wildlife Refuge is a hidden jewel for nature enthusiasts and birdwatchers, located around two hours drive from Richmond. There are hiking and bike paths in this expansive natural region, including a picturesque boardwalk that winds through the center of the swamp. Look out for a range of species, such as otters, black bears, and bald eagles. It offers a tranquil getaway inside a distinctive wetland habitat.

Pocahontas State Park: Accessible Natural Environment

Pocahontas State Park is conveniently located just a short drive from Richmond for those seeking a more convenient day getaway. Hiking, mountain biking, and fishing are just a few of the outdoor activities available in this large park. Hikers love the Beaver Lake Trail because it leads to a gorgeous lake surrounded by dense forest. Families may explore the Nature Center, which offers information on the area's flora and wildlife, and have fun on picnics.

WINERIES AND BREWERIES

The Monticello Wine Trail provides wine connoisseurs with a taste of Virginia's rich winemaking tradition, and it's just a short drive from Richmond. Numerous wineries may be found in Charlottesville and the surrounding region, and many of them provide tastings in picturesque surroundings. A vineyard atop Thomas Jefferson's Monticello, a UNESCO World Heritage site, offers wines that reflect the Founding Fathers' ideas.

Scott's Addition in Richmond: A Mecca for Craft Beer

You won't have to go far if you want craft beer. The Scott's Addition area of Richmond has developed into a center for artisan brewers. Take a brewery tour and stop at well-known locations such as Ardent Craft Ales, Vasen Brewing Company, and The Veil Brewing Co. Savor a wide variety of beer genres, all within a short walking distance from one another, from creamy stouts to hoppy IPAs.

Beautiful Vineyards and Breweries Along the Blue Ridge Parkway

The Blue Ridge Parkway, which provides breathtaking mountain views and a variety of wineries and breweries along the road, is a great destination for a lovely day trip. Visit breweries like Devils Backbone Brewing Company and vineyards like Veritas Vineyard & Winery. A trip you won't soon forget thanks to the amazing vistas and delectable drinks.

Northern Neck Wineries and Breweries — Coastal Wineries

A few hours from Richmond, the Northern Neck area offers vineyards and breweries along the Chesapeake Bay if you'd rather be by the water. Visit locations such as The Dog and Oyster Vineyard for wine tasting, and visit the Heathsville Brewing Company to taste locally brewed artisan brews. In addition, you may enjoy the fresh seafood and see the serene beauty of the bay.

PRACTICAL INFORMATION

HEALTH AND SAFETY TIPS

1. Money and Modes of Payment:

It is crucial to be ready with cash and payment options while organizing your trip to Richmond. Here are some pointers to ensure the security and ease of your banking transactions:

Bring a variety of payment methods: Although credit and debit cards are often accepted in Richmond, it's a good idea to have some cash on hand in case your card is declined or you need to make a minor transaction.

Notify your bank: To prevent possible card holds brought on by suspicious behaviour, let your bank know about your trip intentions before departure.

Currency exchange: If you're going from outside, you should think about converting some money beforehand for convenience, although local banks and ATMs sometimes provide favorable conversion rates.

2. Safety and Health:

Your safety is our priority while visiting Richmond. The following are vital health and safety reminders:

Keep yourself hydrated—the summers in Richmond may be hot and muggy. Reusable water bottles are a great way to remain hydrated, particularly while visiting outdoor sites.

Apply sunscreen: Use sunscreen with a high SPF rating to shield your skin from the sun's rays.

Safety in numbers: Even though Richmond is a fairly safe city, going on an exploration in a group is always a smart idea, particularly in the evening. Keep your valuables safe and pay attention to your surroundings.

Precautions against COVID-19: During your stay, be aware of any health advisories or limitations. Observe mask regulations and keep your distance as needed.

Tips for Eco-Friendly Travel:

1. Cut Down on Your Carbon Imprint:

Traveling sustainably is essential to protecting the environment. Here are some tips for reducing your effect while visiting Richmond:

Take public transportation: There is a good public transportation system in Richmond. Use ridesharing, buses, or trams to lessen your carbon impact.

Ride a bike or stroll: Richmond is a bike-friendly city with plenty of bike lanes and pedestrian-friendly areas. For a sustainable way to see the city, rent a bike or go for a stroll.

2. Promote nearby and environmentally conscious companies:

When you travel sustainably, think about giving a hand to companies that emphasise local sourcing and environmentally beneficial practices:

Farmers' markets: To buy fresh, locally produced products and to support sustainable agriculture, visit your local farmers' market.

Eco-friendly lodgings:

Select lodgings or motels that participate in eco-friendly activities such as energy-saving measures and recycling programs.

3. Cut Down on Plastic Waste:

Richmond has several options for cutting down on plastic trash when traveling:

Reusable products: To cut down on the amount of single-use plastic that is used, bring reusable shopping bags, cutlery, and water bottles.

Eat mindfully by choosing cafés and restaurants that provide takeaway in recyclable or biodegradable containers.

4. Honor regional ecosystems:

It is important to protect Richmond's natural beauty for the coming generations. When making use of its parks and outdoor areas:

Leave no trace: Follow the guidelines of Leave No Trace by packing up everything you own, keeping animal and plant life undisturbed, and not disturbing them.

Follow authorized paths: To preserve delicate ecosystems, stay on routes that have been built.

ITINERARIES

1-DAY HIGHLIGHTS TOUR

Morning:

- Visit the architectural wonder that is the Virginia State Capitol to start your day. Discover Virginia's place in American history by seeing the historic chambers.

- Have breakfast at one of the quaint cafés on Shockoe Slip, like Millie's Diner. Savor a delectable breakfast prepared in the South.

Late in the morning:

- Visit the Virginia Museum of Fine Arts to learn about Richmond's creative side. Discover the vast array of artwork from various parts of the globe.

- Take a stroll around the picturesque Maymont Estate, which has the exquisite Maymont Mansion, Italian gardens, and animal displays.

Lunch:

- Savor a casual lunch at L'Opossum, a restaurant renowned for its inventive American cuisine. Don't miss the creative drinks and distinct atmosphere.

In the afternoon:

- Take a tour of Hollywood Cemetery, the last resting place of several well-known Americans. Discover the histories behind the tombstones by going on a guided tour.

- For an engrossing look at science and technology and interactive displays, visit the Science Museum of Virginia.

Evening:

- Enjoy a lovely supper at The Roosevelt, which specializes in southern-inspired food, to round off your day. Enjoy the regional tastes.

- Before returning to your lodging, take a stroll along the James River Pipeline Walk to take in the picturesque views of the river and downtown Richmond.

3-DAY CULTURAL DEEP DIVE

Day 1: The Art and History of Richmond:

- The American Civil War Museum provides insights into Richmond's participation during the Civil War, so start your cultural journey there.
- Savor lunch at Proper Pie Co., a beloved neighborhood spot serving both sweet and savory pies.
- Explore Virginia's rich history via exhibitions and artifacts at the Virginia Museum of History & Culture throughout the afternoon.

- See a show at the famed Byrd Theatre in the evening; it is renowned for its magnificent architecture and vintage cinema selections.

Day 2: Literature and the Arts

- Begin your day by visiting the Edgar Allan Poe Museum, which honors the life and writings of the well-known author.

- Visit the Virginia Center for Architecture, which showcases the history of the state's architecture.

- Enjoy lunch at the historic Jewish deli Perly's Restaurant & Delicatessen.

- Attend a show at the Virginia Repertory Theatre or spend the day at the Richmond Ballet**.

Day 3: Music and Gardens:

- Start the day by going to the Lewis Ginter Botanical Garden, which is a beautiful green oasis with breathtaking flowers.

- Savor lunch at Stella's, which serves food with a Mediterranean flair.

- Explore Virginia's Black History Museum and Cultural Center in the afternoon, which honors African American history and culture.

- Attend a live music concert at a nearby venue, such as The Broadberry or The National, to round off your cultural immersion.

5-DAY FAMILY ADVENTURE

Day 1: Historical Research

- Visit the Children's Museum of Richmond to begin your family's experience. It offers interactive exhibits and kid-friendly activities.

- Savor a meal at Burger Bach, a family-friendly restaurant renowned for its exquisite burgers.

- Spend the day exploring the Scientific Museum of Virginia, where children may interact with amazing scientific exhibits.

- Grab supper at Bottoms Up Pizza, a well-liked restaurant among pizza enthusiasts.

Day 2: Nature Exploration:

- Take the kids to Maymont Estate for a morning of fun at the nature center and animal displays.

- Paddle boating on Swan Lake after a picnic at Byrd Park.

- See a range of creatures from across the globe by going to the Richmond Metro Zoo in the afternoon.

- Enjoy supper at the entertaining retro-style eatery Galaxy Diner.

Day 3: Fun and History

- Spend the morning seeing the exhibitions of the Virginia Historical Society, which provide historical context for the state.

- Sally Bell's Kitchen, which serves packed lunches, is a good place to have lunch.

Go see more interactive displays and entertaining educational activities at the Science Museum of Virginia.

- Have supper at Mellow Mushroom, which has a laid-back, family-friendly vibe.

Day 4: Environment and Customs

Make an early trip to the Lewis Ginter Botanical Garden, where children may play in the lovely grounds and even a treehouse.

- Enjoy lunch at The Pit and The Peel, a kid-friendly restaurant with a nutritious menu.

- Introduce children to art from across the globe by visiting the Virginia Museum of Fine Arts in the afternoon.

-Enjoy supper while taking in views of the James River from Boathouse at Rocketts Landing.

Day 5: Travel and Parting

Visit Pocahontas State Park first thing in the morning to take advantage of the hiking, picnicking, and nature paths available.

Enjoy a picnic in the park for lunch.

If your family missed any highlights during the trip, spend the day seeing Maymont Estate or the Science Museum of Virginia.

Before leaving back home, have a goodbye meal at a beloved neighborhood restaurant to round off your family's vacation in Richmond.

CONCLUSION

Finally, we would like to say that our trip through the pages of the Richmond Travel Guide has been an amazing experience that has woven a tapestry of memories and feelings that will bind us to this dynamic city forever.

We have investigated Richmond's rich history, creative spirit, and scenic beauty, from the ancient cobblestone alleyways of Shockoe Slip to the verdant gardens of Maymont Estate. We have, at every stage, encouraged a strong emotional connection with this extraordinary location, sensing its pulse and welcoming the kindness of its inhabitants.

Our recollections are filled with unforgettable experiences, such as admiring the breathtaking architecture of the Virginia State Capitol, tasting the distinctive tastes of southern cuisine at L'Opossum, and watching the sunset over the James River from Libby Hill Park.

As we get to the end of our tour, bear the following practical advice in mind: always interact with locals for insider information on hidden jewels; always carry a reusable water bottle for the city's warm days; and explore on foot or by bike to experience the ambiance.

I would want to sincerely thank you, the daring tourist, for making Richmond your destination. Your interest and zeal have added to the significance of our trip.

Our investigation need not stop here, however. Richmond is always changing, with new adventures just around the corner. I urge you to keep exploring this fascinating city, to come back and make new experiences, and to spread the enchantment of Richmond to others.

May you discover inspiration across every corner of our globe, in the spirit of travel and adventure. Continue exploring, traveling, and appreciating the wonder of the uncharted.